The Power of SUNLIGHT

By Joan C. Benson

MODERN CURRICULUM PRESS

Pearson Learning Group

The following people from Pearson Learning Group have contributed to the development of this product:

Art and Design: Dorothea Fox, Jennifer Ribnicky

Editorial: Leslie Feierstone Barna, Nicole Iorio, Patricia Peters

Inventory: Levon Carter

Marketing: Alison Bruno

Production: Roxanne Knoll

ISBN-13: 978-1-4284-1270-5

ISBN-10:   1-4284-1270-0

Printed in the United States of America
1 2 3 4 5 6 7 8 9 10   11 10 09 08 07

Pearson Learning Group

1-800-321-3106
www.pearsonlearning.com

CONTENTS

OUR SUN, OUR EARTH

The Sun has been very important to people ever since the first human beings walked the Earth. Ancient people knew the Sun's light helped their crops grow. Some ancient people feared the coming of winter. Winter days were darker and nights were longer. Shorter, colder days made it harder to grow food and to hunt animals. Ancient people did not know why trees and other plants died in winter. They did not know why the darkness lasted so long.

Today, scientists know that the changing seasons are caused by the way Earth moves around the Sun. Scientists also now understand much more about how sunlight **affects** people, animals, and plants. All living things need sunlight to live. The Sun plays a very important role on Earth.

The Sun is important to all life on Earth.

4

Day and Night

Earth always moves around the Sun. This movement is what creates day and night on Earth. Imagine an orange with a stick through its middle from top to bottom. The stick is the orange's **axis**. You could spin the orange around the stick to see how the Earth moves on its axis. Earth spins around its axis in a similar way to how the orange spins around the stick.

The Earth's axis is not straight up and down. Earth leans, or tilts to the side, as it moves around the Sun. As a result, one part of Earth faces the Sun for more hours a day than other parts of Earth face the Sun.

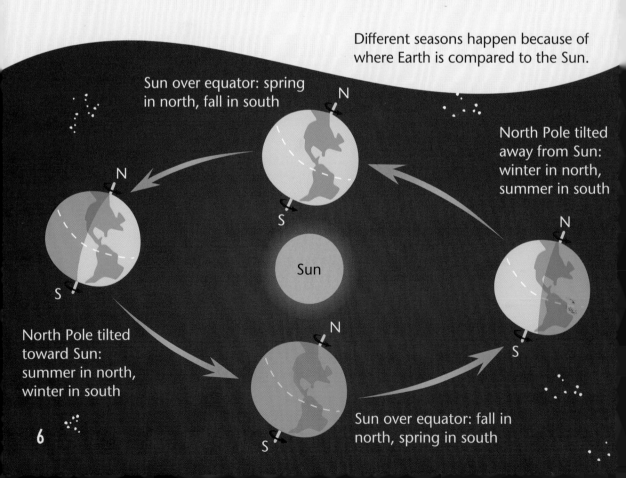

Different seasons happen because of where Earth is compared to the Sun.

Sun over equator: spring in north, fall in south

North Pole tilted away from Sun: winter in north, summer in south

North Pole tilted toward Sun: summer in north, winter in south

Sun

Sun over equator: fall in north, spring in south

Earth is always turning on its axis. It never stops moving. One full turn on Earth's axis takes about 24 hours. This is the amount of time in one day and night on Earth.

Where you live on Earth affects the hours of light you see. When your part of Earth is turned toward the Sun, it is day. When your side of Earth faces away from the Sun, it is night.

Earth's Movement and the Seasons

Earth's movement around the Sun takes about 365 days. That is the length of one year on Earth. When one **hemisphere**, or half of Earth, tilts toward the Sun, it is summer there. The Sun rises early and sets late. At the same time that this part of Earth tilts toward the Sun, the other hemisphere leans away from the Sun. This hemisphere has the shorter, darker, and colder days of winter.

SUN STORIES

The Sun is a star that is 109 times wider than Earth. It would take about 1 million Earths to fill the inside of the Sun!

LIGHT AND PEOPLE

The Sun affects the way your body works. As Earth turns on its axis each day, it brings a new **sunrise** and sunset. Scientists believe that this day and night pattern is built into your body.

Just before daylight, there are changes in your body. Your temperature rises. Your heart beats faster.

Other body systems get ready for the changes a new sunrise brings, too. When morning sunlight enters your eyes, the light sends a **message** to your brain. The brain then sends a message to other systems in your body. This message lets your body know that it is time to be awake and **alert**.

You become more alert as the morning goes on and your systems fully wake up. This is why some scientists believe that late morning is a good time to do work at school. It is natural for your body and mind to be most alert during the day.

The Sun's light helps our minds and bodies wake up.

When it gets dark, your brain sends out a chemical. This chemical makes you feel sleepy. This chemical and the lack of sunlight sends a message to your body. Your body knows to get ready to rest. When you sleep, your heart beats slower. Your body temperature goes down. This time of rest keeps your mind and body **healthy**.

The pattern of Earth's light and dark is like a clock for your body. It helps set times for your body to be awake and to be asleep. However, not all people are able to fit into this natural pattern of light and dark. Some people are in places where there are long periods of either sunlight or darkness. This change in the natural pattern can confuse the clock in people's bodies.

In space, some astronauts find it hard to sleep because of how often they see a sunrise or sunset.

Too Light to Sleep

Astronauts in space cannot tell whether it is morning or night by looking out the windows. They circle Earth at very fast speeds, so there is no pattern of light and dark. In fact, astronauts see a sunrise or a sunset about every 45 minutes when they fly around Earth. Astronauts use their watches so they will not be confused about whether it is day or night.

Astronaut John Phillips has spent more than 190 days in space. In 2005, Phillips lived on the Space Station for six months. Phillips said sleeping at the Space Station was much better than in the space shuttle. At the Space Station, the astronauts could make their own day and night patterns by using inside lights.

The space shuttle was different. It was hard to keep light out of the space shuttle because there were so many windows. Sunlight filled the shuttle about every 45 minutes, and then it was dark for 45 minutes. The astronauts tried covering the windows. Phillips had no problem getting enough sleep. However, some of the astronauts still found it difficult to sleep through the night.

Scientists are working on experiments about how these quick changes in light and dark affect astronauts. The scientists wonder if such quick changes could cause problems. Their experiments will help us learn more about how sleep patterns affect all people.

A World Without Light

Astronauts sometimes do not sleep well because they see too much sunlight. However, not seeing any light can have a similar effect on the body. If you cannot see sunlight at all, your body can also become confused.

Many people who cannot see are sometimes alert when they should be asleep. Like astronauts, they sometimes have trouble sleeping through the night. These people might also suddenly feel sleepy in the middle of the day. This is because light does not enter their eyes in the same way it does for people who can see. As a result, the light does not send messages to the brains and bodies of people who cannot see.

Some places in the far north have two months of darkness in the winter and two months of light in the summer.

If you do not sleep at regular times, your body will slow down. Learning at school or working at a job would then be difficult. Without rest at the right times, your body can also get very tired or weak, and you can get sick.

Winters Without Sun

In some places in the far north, the Sun does not rise during winter for about two months! These long periods of darkness affect the body clocks of people who live in this area. Children in the far north have more trouble in school during the dark months. People do not have as much energy, and they sleep more.

The dark days make some people feel very sad. With light, the brain creates chemicals that help people feel happy. Scientists have discovered that bright lights sometimes help people who live in the far north feel better during the dark days. When the Sun rises again in the spring, these people usually start to feel better on their own.

Vitamins From the Sun

One reason people who live without light for periods of time are often sad is that they are not able to get enough **vitamin** D. When your skin soaks up sunlight, it turns certain chemicals in your body into vitamin D. Scientists have discovered that a lack of vitamin D can make people feel very sad.

A lack of vitamin D can do other things to your body, too. Your bones need vitamin D to grow well and be healthy. In the 1700s and 1800s, many children who lived in crowded cities did not get enough sunlight. Tall buildings shaded the streets where they played. Dirty air did not let the light pass through. Without enough light, the children's bones did not get enough vitamin D from the Sun. Their bones became soft and bent. They could not grow tall and strong. People began to add vitamin D to milk and food to help with this problem.

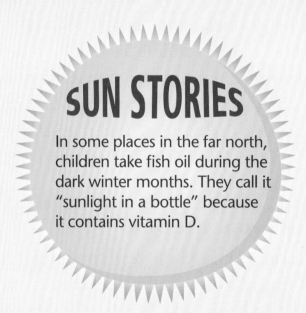

SUN STORIES

In some places in the far north, children take fish oil during the dark winter months. They call it "sunlight in a bottle" because it contains vitamin D.

Drinking milk that has vitamin D added to it can help keep your bones strong.

LIGHT AND ANIMALS

Animals, like people, are very much affected by the amount of sunlight they get. Like the people who live in the far north, penguins in the cold and icy far south have long weeks of darkness and long weeks of light. These birds build their nests, choose their mates, and eat a lot when the days are long.

When the Sun shines for more hours, it keeps the temperatures in the far south a little warmer. Longer days also make it easy for penguins to hunt for food. Penguin babies have a better chance of living if they hatch when there is more food and warmer temperatures.

During this time of long days, penguins eat a lot. Eating a lot of food helps the penguins store up fat in their body. Without fat, penguins would not be able to live through the dark and cold months ahead when there is less food.

When the sunlight hours are short and there is darkness for weeks, penguins do not swim and play. Even their eating slows down in these darker periods. The penguins crowd close together during this time. They have to save their energy and keep warm in temperatures that can sometimes be as low as –125 degrees!

Penguins have their babies at the time of year when the days are long.

Other animals have a different way of living with shorter days and longer nights. Some animals, such as one kind of ground squirrel in the far north, hibernate. Animals that hibernate sleep for many months.

In the long days of summer, ground squirrels eat a lot of food and store up a lot of fat. When the days become shorter, the ground squirrel gets ready for the seven or eight months it will be asleep. These squirrels eat almost no food the entire time they hibernate.

As the squirrels hibernate, their bodies go through many changes. Their body temperature falls below 32 degrees, which is the temperature at which water turns to ice! The squirrels also breathe slower. They can breathe as few as two times per minute.

In spring, the days begin to get longer again. The ground squirrels wake up. The longer days help their bodies know when it is time to wake up and be alert.

SUN STORIES

When ground squirrels wake from their deep sleep, their hearts begin to beat faster and they breathe faster. The process of waking up takes them about three hours.

This ground squirrel will hibernate like this for more than half a year.

LIGHT AND PLANTS

Imagine what it would be like if your body could create its own food. Plants can create their own food, but they cannot do it alone. They must have sunlight. Using the Sun's energy to make food is not a simple process. It begins when sunlight hits the green part of a plant. Plants also need water as well as a special gas from the air. The sunlight, gas, water, and plant all work together to create food for the plant.

When plants are done making their food, they give off **oxygen**. People and animals cannot live without oxygen. Almost all the oxygen we breathe has been made by the Sun working together with plants.

These flowers are turning
to face the Sun.

Sometimes, plants' flowers and stems lean toward the Sun. This happens because of a chemical in plants that always moves to the shady side of the stems. The chemical makes the stems grow faster and taller on the shady side. Then the shorter side of the stem makes the plant lean toward the sunlight.

The number of hours of sunlight during the day also affects plants. Long days of sunlight tell plants that it is time for their flowers to bloom. The shorter days of fall tell plants that it is time for their leaves to die and drop off. Long nights in the winter make tree buds rest. The buds begin to develop into leaves when the days become longer again.

Some plants have day and night patterns, too. Some flowers open with the morning Sun and close up as night comes. The leaves on bean plants rise toward the Sun at a regular time each day. Some plant leaves droop or hang down and fold up in the evening.

SUN STORIES

Many plants are needed to produce oxygen. To keep a person alive for an hour, about 300 to 400 plants are needed.

THE SUN'S POWER

The Sun is Earth's closest star. Even though this star is 93 million miles away from Earth, nothing in our world gives off more light than the Sun. In its early days, the Sun was not as bright as it is today. The Sun, even then, gave enough light and heat so that Earth did not freeze. However, if there were no Sun, everything on Earth would freeze and die.

The Sun has been giving us light and heat for 4.5 billion years. Scientists expect that the Sun will continue to give us light and heat for another 5 billion years. The amount of light that we get can change over time, and certainly over billions of years. These changes affect the lives of people, animals, and plants on Earth. The changes also affect the seasons. Scientists who study the Sun look at these changes and how they affect Earth.

We have come a long way in our understanding of the Sun and how it affects life on Earth. We know that it affects the seasons. We know that the Sun affects sleep patterns. We understand its power. Today, we know that the Sun and Earth work together to keep people, animals, and plants healthy.

Day and night affect life on Earth.

GLOSSARY

affects does something to

alert fully awake and able to act quickly

astronauts people who travel to and in space

axis the line on which Earth turns every 24 hours

healthy free of pain and sickness; feeling well

hemisphere half of the Earth

message information sent from one place to another

oxygen a gas in the air that people and animals breathe in order to live

sunrise the time when the Sun enters the sky in the morning

vitamin something that helps to keep the body healthy